Baba Yaga, I have to tell you, is a bad witch. She travels a lot, but you can find her most often in Russian, Czech and Polish fairy tales. Sometimes she appears as a thunder witch – the devil's grandmother. She is an ugly old woman with a monstrous nose and long teeth. Her hair is a frightful mess, and sometimes, in the worst cases, she eats boys and girls for dinner! There she'll be (after dinner!) flying through the sky in an iron cauldron, sweeping her traces from the air with a broom.

Each writer who has the courage to tackle Baba Yaga adds their own little deadly touches. We hope you like ours. We hope they give you the shivers!

ANNA FIENBERG

Anna and Barbara Fienberg write the Tashi stories together, making up all kinds of daredevil adventures and tricky characters for him to face. Lucky he's such a clever Tashi.

Kim Gamble is one of Australia's favourite illustrators for children. Together Kim and Anna have made such wonderful books as *The Magnificent Nose and Other Marvels*, *The Hottest Boy Who Ever Lived*, the *Tashi* series, the *Minton* picture books, *Joseph*, and a full colour picture book about their favourite adventurer, *There once was a boy called Tashi.*

Anna Fienberg would like to thank the Literature Board of the Australia Council for their assistance.

First published in the English Language by Allen & Unwin Pty Ltd, Sydney, Australia.

First Indian Edition 2010

VIVA BOOKS PRIVATE LIMITED

- 4737/23 Ansari Road, Daryaganj, New Delhi 110 002
  E-mail: vivadelhi@vivagroupindia.net, Tel. 42242200
- 76, Service Industries, Shirvane, Sector 1, Nerul, Navi Mumbai 400 706
  E-mail: vivamumbai@vivagroupindia.net, Tel. 27721273, 27721274
- Jamals Fazal Chambers, 26 Greams Road, Chennai 600 006
  E-mail: vivachennai@vivagroupindia.net, Tel. 28290304, 28294241
- B-103, Jindal Towers, 21/1A/3 Darga Road, Kolkata 700 017
  E-mail: vivakolkata@vivagroupindia.net, Tel. 22836381, 22816713
- 7, Sovereign Park Apartments, 56-58, K. R. Road, Basavanagudi, Bangalore 560 004
  E-mail: vivabangalore@vivagroupindia.net, Tel. 26607409, 26607410
- 101-102 Mughal Marc Apartments, 3-4-637 to 641, Narayanguda, Hyderabad 500 029
  E-mail: vivahyderabad@vivagroupindia.net, Tel. 27564481, 27564482
- First Floor, Beevi Towers, SRM Road, Kaloor, Kochi 682 018, Kerala
  E-mail: vivakochi@vivagroupindia.net, Tel: 0484-2403055, 2403056
- 232, GNB Road, Beside UCO Bank, Silpukhuri, Guwahati 781 003
  E-mail: vivaguwahati@vivagroupindia.net, Tel: 0361-2666386

www.vivagroupindia.com

Published by arrangement with:
Allen & Unwin
83 Alexander St
Crows Nest NSW 2065
Australia

ISBN : 978-81-309-1327-8

Published by Vinod Vasishtha for Viva Books Private Limited, 4737/23, Ansari Road, Daryaganj, New Delhi-110 002. Printed and bound by Swan Press, New Delhi.

Tashi and the BABA YAGA

written by
Anna Fienberg
and
Barbara Fienberg

illustrated by
Kim Gamble

Viva Books
New Delhi | Mumbai | Chennai | Kolkata | Bangalore | Hyderabad | Kochi | Guwahati

JACK'S DAD SAT up in bed reading the newspaper. He had a cold, and his tissue box was nearly empty. '"Beach Houses For Sale",' Dad read aloud. 'How would you like to move to a house near the beach, Jack?' He blew his nose. 'Just imagine—an early morning swim, watching the sun rise over the sea. Look at this one—a nice little wooden house, with plenty of personality.'

'Looks as big as a beehive to me,' said Jack. 'Anyway, I like it *here*—near all my friends. Besides,' Jack narrowed his eyes and tapped the side of his nose slyly, 'you've got to be careful about exploring new houses. You never know what you may find inside.'

Dad put down his paper. 'Really?' He smoothed a place on the bed for Jack to come and sit down. He rubbed his hands together. Yes, he could definitely feel a story coming on—one of Jack's Tashi stories, no doubt. Since young Tashi had moved into the neighbourhood, and become best friends with Jack, they'd heard some amazing adventures.

'I suppose your friend Tashi knows all about new houses?' said Dad.

'Yes, when he was back in the old country, a new house did arrive in his village one day.'

'Arrive?' repeated Dad, puzzled. 'How could a house *arrive*? No, wait a second. MUM,' called Dad, 'MU-UM, come and listen to a story!' He grinned at Jack. 'She'd be so cross if she missed out.'

Mum came panting into the room, her arms full of dirty washing. She plonked it on the floor and curled up next to Dad.

'Wacko!' she cried. She glanced scornfully at the washing. 'That can wait. So, what's it all about?'

'Well, it was like this,' Jack began, and he shivered as he remembered Tashi's words of last night. 'Baba Yaga blew in to Tashi's village on the winds of a terrible storm.'

'Baba Yaga? Who is that?' coughed Dad. 'Someone looking for a new house?'

'Pay attention and you'll find out,' said Jack.

'And don't breathe on me,' said Mum.

'Well, one night, when Tashi was quite small, stinging rains lashed the village and wild winds blew washing off the lines and chickens out of their nests. Branches were torn from the trees and whole houses were whisked miles away.

'The next morning, when Tashi walked along the road, he saw people scurrying about trying to find lost belongings that had been scattered far and wide. He offered to help and, going further and further from the village, he found cooking pots and slippers high up in the trees.

'Because he was looking up, he almost stepped on a raven that was pinned under a fallen branch. Tashi gently lifted the bird from the leaves and twigs and placed it on a grassy mound. The bird was very weak and thirsty so Tashi gave it a drink of water from his bottle.

'"Thank you," said the raven. "You have been my friend. Maybe one day *I* will be able to help *you*."'

'Ho *ho*,' crowed Dad, and blew his nose like a trumpet.

'Well,' Jack went on, 'as Tashi walked on through the forest, he came upon a house in a clearing where there had been no house before. And what an extraordinary house it was! It stood on scaly yellow chicken legs, and the claws dug deep into the earth. Above, a thread of crooked smoke rose out of a crooked chimney.'

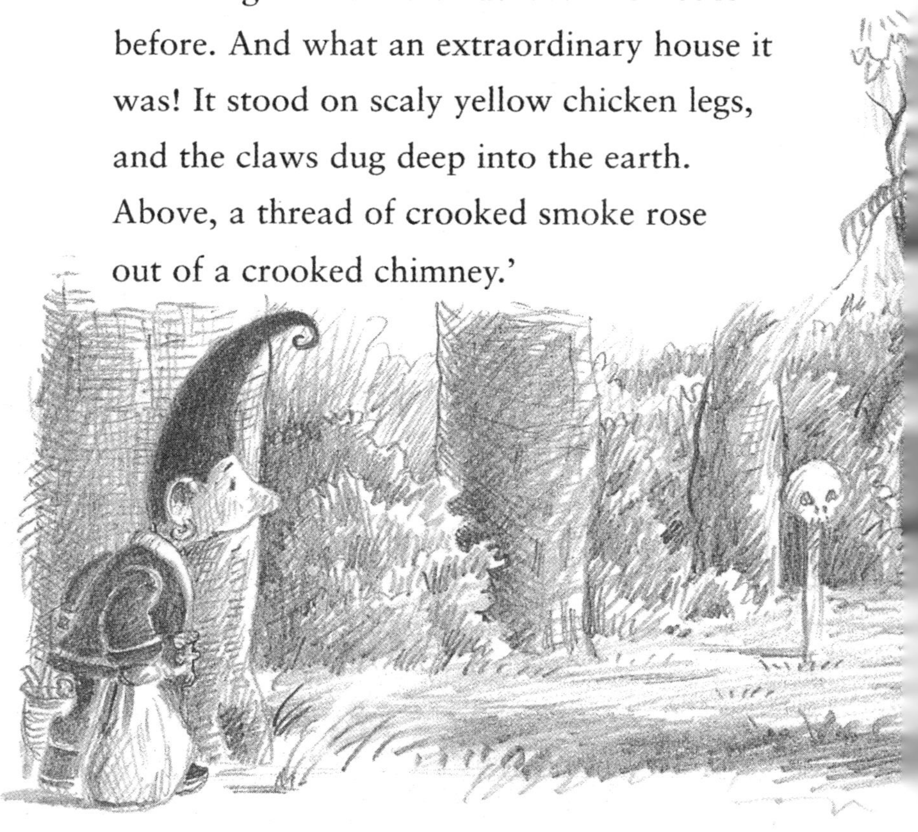

'Hmm!' Dad wrinkled his nose. 'Just like the newspaper said—a nice little wooden house with plenty of personality!'

'Ugh! Did Tashi dare to peep inside?' asked Mum.

'Well,' said Jack, 'it was like this. He put down all his bundles and crept closer. He wanted to see more, but was a bit afraid. And then, suddenly, the door opened and an old woman stepped outside.

'"Aha, our first visitor has arrived, Alenka," she crowed to a young girl who came to the window. "Won't you come in and tell us all about yourself while you have a glass of tea?"

'Tashi hesitated for a moment, but he was so eager to explore this weird house that he thanked her and followed her inside.

'There was an enormous stove in one corner of the room and nearby, on a stool, lay a half-plucked goose. Sticky feathers and smears of blood covered the young girl's hands.

'As he sipped his tea, Tashi asked the old woman how it was that her house had appeared so suddenly in the forest. The old woman leaned towards Tashi and looked into his face. "My name is Baba Yaga," she rasped, "and I come from a land far, far away. The storm blew me right over the mountains, into this forest. But I don't think I'll stay here. It seems a dismal sort of place to me, not many children about." Her voice scraped like sandpaper on wood. Her black eyes pierced Tashi's own. Then she reached over and pinched his arm. "You look a nice juicy boy however, and if there's one thing I do enjoy, it's Boy-Baked-In-A-Pie."

'Tashi could hardly believe his ears; did she really mean it, or was she just teasing?'
'Probably just teasing,' Dad said heartily. Then he looked at Jack's face and gulped.
'Wasn't she?'
'Go on, Jack,' said Mum. 'What happened next?'

'Well,' said Jack, 'it was like this. Tashi was staring at her, half-smiling and hoping she was joking, when suddenly she smiled back. He gasped in horror. Her teeth were made of iron!

'He looked around wildly and saw, through the window, that the sun had vanished behind the clouds. The fence posts glowed white against the dark sky. Tashi peered closer. His heart thumped and he bit his lip, hard. On top of each post sat a small skull—a child's-size skull—with a candle lit inside it. "Wah!" he screamed.

'Baba Yaga leapt up. "Take the boy," she roared at her daughter, "and get him ready for baking. We'll have a fine meal tonight!" And she hobbled out into the forest to gather some herbs and mushrooms.

'Alenka dragged Tashi over to the oven. Her strong fingers bit down through his jacket like claws. With one hand she built up the fire, then dropped Tashi onto the oven spade, as if he were nothing but a loaf of bread.

‘Quick, he thought, what can I do? He gazed longingly through the open door, and spied an old apple tree. *Aha!* His heart leapt with hope.

‘“Don’t you use apples and spice when you roast m-meat?” he asked. “Everyone in my village says that it makes a dish much tastier.”

‘“Does it now?” said Alenka. “I’ll try it then.”

'And she strode out of the room and down the steps to gather some apples in her apron, bolting the door behind her.

'Quick as lightning, Tashi pulled off his jacket and trousers and shoes and put them on the goose that was left lying on the stool in the corner. He stood back for a second to look. Wasn't something missing? Of course: the goose-boy needed some hair.

'*Hurry hurry*, yes, that would do. He snatched up a black sock that Alenka had been knitting and unravelled some wool. When he had arranged it with the curl over the goose's "face", it looked so real that Tashi felt a bit sick. He just had time to hide in the cupboard before Alenka came back.

'"That was a good idea of yours, Tashi,"
she said as she stuck some cloves in the apples. She pushed one apple up each leg and arm of the goose-boy's trousers and jacket, and then slid the oven spade right into the red heart of the oven.

‘Inside his cupboard, Tashi trembled. He heard the oven door slam, and soon the smell of cooking crept in through the cracks of the wooden cupboard.

‘When Baba Yaga came back, she scolded Alenka for not waiting for the mushrooms. ‘“Great greedy gizzards, why don’t you do as I tell you? Boy-Baked-In-A-Pie needs mushrooms, and *you* need your brains boiled!”

'But the old woman stopped finding fault when she sniffed the delicious smells coming from the oven.

'"Apples and cloves," Alenka announced proudly. "Tashi told me how to do it."

'They sat down at the table and began to eat. Baba Yaga chewed on a small piece of leg, and smacked her lips. "This dinner is quite tasty," she said grudgingly. She paused a moment.'

'For a burp, I bet,' said Dad. 'A woman like that would have no manners.'

'Tashi didn't mention any burping,' replied Jack. 'Anyway, *then* the old woman began to look suspiciously at the meat. She poked it with her fork. "This looks like goose." She paused again. "It smells like goose. It *is* goose!"

'The old woman stood up and pointed her craggy finger at Alenka. "You stupid, snail-witted lump! Can't you do anything right? Now where did that Tashi get to? You stay here and search the house while I see if he ran to the village."

'Alenka got down on her hands and knees and looked under the bed. She looked behind the screen and then she turned towards the cupboard. Through the crack in the door, Tashi could see her moving towards him. He began to shake. In the tight, dark space of the cupboard he could hardly breathe.

'But then he saw something else. There, across the room, sitting on the windowsill was his friend, the raven.

'"Are you looking for something?" the bird called.

'"Yes," said Alenka. "A juicy boy that was supposed to have been our dinner."

'"Ah," nodded the raven. "I saw such a boy hiding in the garden just now."

'"Good!" Alenka shouted, and she ran down the steps to catch Tashi.

'Quickly Tashi slipped out of the cupboard. He whispered, "Thank you!" to the raven as he clambered out the window. Then he ran through the forest, with the trees moaning in the wind and the storm clouds racing across the sky and a rusty old voice calling on the air like a crow at dusk.

'The next morning Tashi's mother was very cross that he had lost all his clothes. When Tashi told her that Baba Yaga had cooked them, thinking he was inside them, she didn't quite believe him.

'"Come, I'll show you," said Tashi, and he led her into the forest. The strange house was still there, standing on its bony old chicken feet. And the crooked smoke was still drifting out of the crooked chimney.

'Tashi's mother shivered, and drew him close to her. "What did I tell you?" said Tashi.

'But just then, while they were both still staring, the house rose up high on its legs and scurried out of the forest, flying over the mountains and away, never to be seen in Tashi's village again.'

Jack's parents were silent for a moment, thinking. Then Dad sneezed.

'Ugh!' he shivered. 'I hope that house doesn't blow anywhere near *here*. No one would want a place like that, even if they were selling it for chicken feed.'

Jack leapt off the bed with a grin. 'Funny you should mention *chickens*, Dad, because they were the cause of Tashi's next problem.'

'Well, the worst thing about chickens is chicken poo,' said Dad. 'That might be a smelly problem, but how could it be *dangerous*?'

'You'll see this afternoon,' Jack called over his shoulder as he ran out of the room. 'Tashi's coming over and he'll tell you himself!'

'Is it the afternoon yet?' asked Dad, who didn't know what time it was since he'd been in bed.

'No, not for hours,' Jack called back.

Dad groaned, and flopped back on the pillow.

At four o'clock Jack met Tashi at the garden gate.

'Sorry I'm late,' panted Tashi, 'but three of our chickens escaped through a hole in the fence and we had to chase them to the creek and back. Pesky things!'

Tashi wiped his feet on the mat. Jack looked down curiously at Tashi's boots, and sniffed.

'Perhaps I'd better leave them outside,' said Tashi.

'Perhaps,' agreed Jack.

'So,' said Jack, when they were sitting comfortably, 'did you get all three chickens back?'

'Oh yes,' said Tashi, 'but I remember a time when it wasn't so easy. Once, every hen in our village disappeared. Nothing was left behind—not even a feather floating in the air.'

'How dreadful,' said Mum, coming into the room. 'What did you do for eggs?'

'Well,' said Tashi, stretching out his legs, 'it was like this.'

'Wait,' cried Jack. 'Dad's still asleep. Fair's fair.' He scrambled upstairs, flung open his father's door, and shouted 'BABA YAGA!' Dad screamed and shot out of bed as if the witch was swooping through the window right behind him.

He was still breathing heavily when he was settled on the sofa with a rug over his knees. He stared at Tashi. 'I don't know how you could even look at chickens again after Baba Yaga,' he said, and sneezed.

'Hmm,' Tashi nodded, 'but a man has to eat. When all the hens disappeared, no one in the village had a clue where they could be. People were grizzling because they had to start work without their omelettes. They invented excuses to poke about in each other's houses, but they found nothing.

'One day my mother threw down her spoon and said she was tired of trying to cook without eggs. She sent me over to Third Aunt, who worked as a cook for the wicked Baron. Since he was the richest man in the village, she thought that perhaps he might have a few eggs left.'

'Oh I remember *him*!' cried Dad. 'He was that rascal who kept all his money on a mountain—'

'Guarded by a pack of white tigers,' shuddered Mum.

'Yes,' agreed Tashi. 'He had the heart of a robber, and the smile of a snake, and I didn't like going near him. But what else could I do? I set off at once and on the way I met Cousin Wu. He had just returned from a trip to the city, and he couldn't stop talking about the wonders he'd seen there. "The best thing of all," he said, "was the Flying Fireball Circus. You should have seen it, Tashi—the jugglers and the acrobats on the high trapeze—I couldn't believe my eyes."

'"You are lucky, Wu," I sighed. "I don't suppose we will ever see a circus here. The village would never have enough money to pay for one to visit."

'We walked along in silence for a while, and then I asked Cousin Wu if he wanted to come with me to the Baron's house. Suddenly he seemed to be in a great hurry to visit his sister, so we said goodbye and I went on my way.

'Unfortunately, just as I was opening the gate to the Baron's house, the wicked man himself leant out the window and saw me. "Be off with you, you little worm," he shouted. "I don't want to see you hanging about my house!"'

'Worm—*he's* the worm,' said Dad crossly. 'Someone ought to squish him!'

'Well,' Tashi went on, 'I pretended to run off home, but as soon as the Baron closed his shutters, I ducked back into the kitchen where Third Aunt had made some delicious sticky sweet rice cakes, my favourite. When I had wolfed down five or six, I remembered the eggs.

'"Of course you can have some," said Third Aunt. "We have plenty. More than we know what to do with, in fact."

'"Have you?" I said. "That's very interesting." And I followed her outside to an enormous shed and waited while she unlocked the door. And do you know what? I found hundreds of hens—and some of them were my old friends! I recognised Gong Gong's Pullet and Second Cousin's big Peking Red.

‘“Don’t wait for me,” I told Third Aunt. “I’ll fill this bowl and be out in a minute.” When she left, I walked amongst the birds and made sure that all the village hens were there in the Baron’s chicken house. Then I sniffed the smell of cigars. Strange, I thought. Cigar smoke in a chicken house? I sniffed again and the skin on my neck tingled. Slowly I turned around. And there, in the doorway blocking the light, stood the wicked Baron.

'He marched inside and closed the door behind him. "So, little worms wriggle into peculiar places," he said with a nasty sneer. "But can they wriggle out again, I wonder?"

'"You have stolen all our chickens!" I cried. "Why? Whatever are you going to do with them?"

'"That is none of your business . . . but then, maybe I'll tell you since you won't be here long enough to do anything about it." And he grinned, showing all his glinting gold teeth. "I am going to sell half of them to the River Pirate, who'll be sailing past this house at midnight. Then tomorrow, I'll be able to charge whatever I like for my eggs because no one else will have any to sell. I'll make a fortune! Golden eggs, they'll be! What do you think of that, little worm?"

'I stared at him. It was hard to believe anyone could be so mean.'

'I know,' agreed Dad, nodding his head. 'The newspapers are full of crooks getting away with it. Makes your blood boil.'

'Well, I was determined *he* wouldn't get away with it. I edged toward the door. "You can't keep me here," I told him, thinking I could make a dash for it.

‘The Baron laughed fiercely. It sounded like a growl. “Oh no, little fish bait, I have plans for you. I will lock you up in the storeroom until midnight, when the River Pirate will take *you* as well as the hens. A pirate’s prisoner, that’s what you’ll be!” And he grabbed me and threw me over his shoulder like a bit of old rope, and dropped me into the cold, dark storeroom.

'At first, there was just darkness, and silence. But as my eyes grew used to the gloom, I saw the walls were thick stone, and a square of grey light shone in through one small high window. I felt all round the heavy iron door, but it was padlocked, as tight as a treasure chest. I bent down to study the floor, to see if there were any trapdoors, or loose stones. And it was then that I saw it. Lying in the corner, curled up like a wisp of smoke, was a white tiger.'

'The Baron's tiger!' screamed Jack. 'What did you do?'

'Well, it was like this. I just stayed where I was and made no sound. I could see that its eyes were closed. Its legs twitched now and then, as if it were chasing something in a dream. It was asleep, but for how long? I put my head in my hands. There was no way out. I felt like a fly in a web. Only *my* web was made of solid stone.

'If only I had my magic ghost cakes, I thought. I could walk through that wall, as easily as walking through air. I searched in my empty pockets. Wait! There was a small crumb. But would it be enough to get me all the way through those thick walls? Should I take the chance?'

'Yes, yes!' cried Jack.

Tashi nodded. 'I put the crumb on my tongue and as I swallowed I began to push through the stone. My right foot first—it was gliding through!—and then I stopped. The rest of my leg was stuck fast, deep inside the stone.

'I moaned aloud. Over my shoulder I saw the tiger stir. I saw one eye open. Then the other. I'd forgotten the colour of those eyes: red, like coals of fire. The tiger growled deep in its throat. It made me think of the Baron, and how he would laugh to see me trapped like this. Slowly, lazily, the tiger uncurled itself.

'I scrabbled through my top pockets. Nothing. I was frantic. The tiger was padding towards me. It leaned back on its haunches, ready to spring. It was hard to look away from its snarling mouth, but yes, there in the very last pocket of all, I felt something soft and squashy. Another cake crumb!

'I swallowed the crumb as the tiger sprang. Its jaws opened and a spiky whisker swiped my hand, but I was away, slipping through the stone as easily as a fish noodle slips down your throat.

'Outside it was cool and breezy, and I stretched my arms out wide and did a little dance of freedom. Then I saw Cousin Wu, coming back from his sister's. I ran to him and told him, in a great rush, what the Baron had done.

'"That thieving devil!" cried Cousin Wu. "I'd like to drop him down a great black hole, down to the burning centre of the earth! But first, let's go and tell the village."

'"You go," I said, "but just say to everyone that you've discovered who stole the hens—nothing more. There is something I have to do here first."'

'What?' cried Dad, hanging on to his blanket.

Tashi smiled. 'I had other plans for the Baron. You see, it was almost midnight. I hurried down to the Baron's jetty, to wait for the River Pirate. The moon was up, and soon I heard the soft *shush shush* of the motor. The boat came around the bend, riding the moon's path of silver. The Pirate tied up at the jetty, and stepped out.

'He was tall and looked as strong as ten lions. I didn't fancy being taken as his prisoner, but still I went to meet him. "I have some news from the Baron," I began. "He has changed his mind about selling you the hens."

'The River Pirate frowned. It was a terrible

frown, and I noticed him stroke the handle of his sword. Quickly I added, “But I have something for you.” I drew out of my pocket a small bag of “gold” that a tricky genie had given me some time ago. “The Baron said that this is for your trouble.”

‘Well, the River Pirate stopped frowning, and clapped me on the back.

'In the distance I could see a large crowd of people marching from the village. They were waving flaming torches high above their heads, shouting fiercely. And there was the Baron coming out of his house, on his way down to meet the River Pirate. He hurried over to see what all the smoke and noise was about, and when he saw me, he gasped with surprise.

'I walked up to him and said sternly, "Here come the villagers. Can you see how angry they are? How furious? You have two choices. Either I will tell them how you stole their hens—and who knows what they will do to you, with their flaming torches and fiery tempers." The Baron turned pale in the moonlight.

'"Or?" he asked. "What about the *or*?"

'"Or," I said slowly, stretching out the word like a rubbery noodle, "I can tell them you discovered that the River Pirate had stolen their hens, and, as an act of kindness, you bought the hens back for them."

'The Baron gave a great growl of relief. "That's the one I like, Tashi, my boy!"

'But I hadn't finished. "And you will invite them all to see the wonderful Flying Fireball Circus, which you will bring here to the village next week."

'"The circus? Are you mad? You sneaky little worm, that would cost me a fortune!" roared the Baron.

'"Yes," I agreed. "Don't those flames look splendid against the black sky?"

'And when the Baron turned to see, the villagers were almost upon us. "WHERE IS THE THIEF! WHERE IS THE THIEF!" they chanted.'

'And did the villagers set upon him with their fiery tempers?' Dad asked eagerly.

'No,' Tashi smiled. 'We all went to see the acrobats and the jugglers and the daredevil horsemen at the circus, and we had the best night of our lives.'

'So,' Dad sighed, 'I suppose everyone had eggs for breakfast from then on and talked about the circus over tea, and Cousin Wu saw a lot of his sister.'

'Yes,' agreed Tashi, 'life was quite peaceful—for a while. Hey, Jack,' Tashi turned to his friend, 'let's go out into the garden and play Baba Yaga.'

'Okay,' said Jack. 'I'll be the witch and you can be the dinner,' and they raced outside to the peppercorn tree.

Dad went back to bed.